Veiled
in truth, goodness, and beauty

An Interactive Workbook for Catholic Women
With the Vocation of Marriage & Motherhood

Participant Edition

Kira G. King

Originally published in Savannah, Georgia by Wymberly Communications

www.kiragking.com

ISBN: 979-8-218-64689-9

Foreward

When I was asked to write the Foreword for the *Veiled* workbook, I had no idea the impact it would have on me. As a writer and publisher, I read several manuscripts a week. But this one made me ponder how different my life would have been if this resource had been available to me in high school. What if every woman was encouraged to develop into the best version of herself? Sounds dreamy, right? Well, guess what? That's exactly what's in store for you!

As you embark on this journey, you'll find that traditional schooling may not reveal the true treasure of your unique identity. While the subjects of math, science, and English fill pages, they often overlook the deeper exploration of who you are and what you're capable of becoming. This workbook is a life-changing tool for discovering your natural, God-given talents while diving into the rich teachings of the Catechism of the Catholic Church. Prepare to delve into your innermost thoughts and feelings as you uncover the remarkable treasures that lie within.

I've had the front-row seat to witness the amazing journey of the author, Kira King. She was once a curious teen in the Catholic small-group program my husband and I hosted. With an insatiable thirst for knowledge, she asked questions that challenged us. This spirit of inquiry paved the way for her to create a path that invites you to explore, grow, and connect with your divine purpose.

I encourage you to embrace your curiosity without restraint as you turn the pages, think outside the box, and never stop asking God to guide you as you navigate this adventure of self-discovery and happiness. The best is yet to come, and your adventure is just beginning!

Leigh Ebberwein

Saint Vincent's Academy Graduate, Wife, Mother of Seven Children, Author of *The Saints of Savannah Series*, & Publisher at Old Fort Press

Dear Sister In Christ,

I am excited to share this treasure chest of Catholic riches with you. The pages that lie before you are full of scripture, Church teachings, Saints' quotes, priests' writings, activities, fun crafts, and thought-provoking prompts. Most importantly, however, this workbook is designed for *you*.

It is for you in this moment, in this chapter, in this season of your life, whether you are not yet married but wish to be, have been married for a short time, or have years of marriage behind you. You are invited to a life of sanctity by the Holy Spirit. You are desired by Jesus Christ to live in communion with Him. You are cherished and loved by our almighty Father. You are called to a vocation.

The pages before you are not a fast-track highway. They are a meandering and fruitful path with small, sometimes painful, bumps along the way. Some areas in this journey will be like a welcomed hug, giving you rest and comfort. Others may challenge you and may even bring you to a place of anger or hurt. Still, others will help you to gaze inward and strive for growth. Our path to holiness is the narrow road, less traveled. It is not glamorous. It is not easy, but it is so much more.

You, sister in Christ, are called to **more**. You are called to be a <u>SAINT</u>! We all are.

As we take this walk together, I ask that you pray to the Holy Spirit to open your mind and heart to the truth of scripture, the beauty of the Catechism of the Catholic Church, the goodness of the Saints, the guidance of our priests, and the dignity and worth of you, your (future) spouse and family, and all those around you. Know of my continued prayers for you. Please pray for me too.

With all my love,

Kira

How the Workbook Works

What You'll Need:

1. Colored markers, pens, and/or pencils *(for writing & doodling)*
2. Access to the Catechism of the Catholic Church *(can be found for free online)*
3. A Catholic version of the Bible *(can be found for free online)*
4. *Veiled In Goodness* by Kira G. King

How It Works

- There are eight sections, each with eight segments. A facilitator or teacher will help walk you through each section.
    - 01- Featured Catechism of the Catholic Church paragraphs
        - *If you choose to go through the workbook without a facilitator, please spend ample time in 01 to adequately prepare you for the remaining segments.*
    - 02-03- Interactive Activities
    - 04- Featured quote with suggested future reading
    - 05- Discussion Questions *(whole group or in small groups)*
    - 06- Creation Crafting *(whole group or individually)*
    - 07 - Word Study *(individually)*
    - 08- Featured article written exclusively for **you** by a priest.
- Some scripture passages are provided for you. Others are referenced so that you may look them up.

Think of this workbook as your own piece of art. Write your thoughts and answers in a colorful array all over the pages. Don't worry about how it looks. Just enjoy the process!

CORRESPONDING READINGS

This workbook is designed to be a companion to *Veiled In Goodness: A Catholic Guide For Young Women Seeking Marriage and Motherhood* by Kira G. King. Below are the corresponding readings for each section of the workbook. Please read each assigned reading *before* diving into its section in the workbook.

Workbook	Veiled In Goodness
Section I ->	Prologue + Chapter 1 + Responses & Q&A
Section II ->	Chapter 2 + Responses & Q&A
Section III ->	Chapter 3 + Responses & Q&A
Section IV ->	Chapters 4-5 + Responses & Q&A
Section V ->	Chapter 6
Section VI ->	Chapter 7 + Responses & Q&A
Section VII ->	Chapter 8 + Responses & Q&A
Section VIII ->	Chapter 9 + Epilogue

I believe...

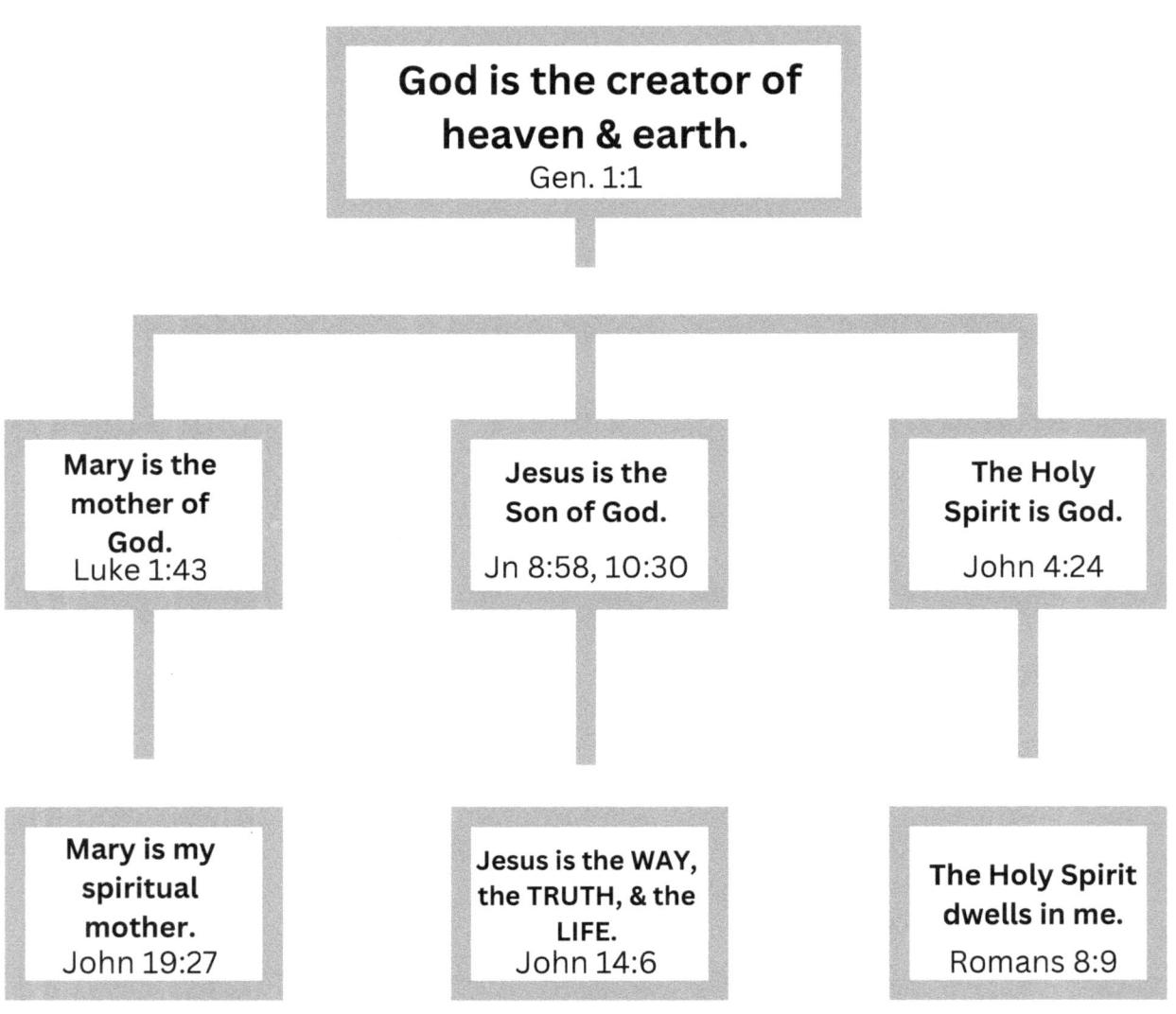

God is the creator of heaven & earth.
Gen. 1:1

Mary is the mother of God.
Luke 1:43

Jesus is the Son of God.
Jn 8:58, 10:30

The Holy Spirit is God.
John 4:24

Mary is my spiritual mother.
John 19:27

Jesus is the WAY, the TRUTH, & the LIFE.
John 14:6

The Holy Spirit dwells in me.
Romans 8:9

From this point on, we understand these truths as universal.

Section I
Prayer

01 What is Prayer?

Find these paragraphs in the Catechism of the Catholic Church, read along, and listen closely as your facilitator focuses on key points.

Topic	Catechism
1. God's Gift	1. CCC 2559, 2560, 2561
2. Covenant	2. CCC 2562-2564
3. Communion	3. CCC 2565
4. Foundation	4. CCC 2654-2655
5. Sacrifice	5. CCC 2659, 2728, 2749

GOAL OF PRAYER
=
LOVING RELATIONSHIP WITH TRINITY

Catechism Notes

Write down your individual notes as you listen to or read along with the Catechism of the Catholic Church.

Prayer as God's Gift CCC 2559-2561

Prayer As Covenant CCC 2562-2564

Prayer As Communion CCC 2565

Prayer As Foundation CCC 2654-2655

Prayer As Sacrifice CCC 2659, 2728, 2749

02 How to Pray?

THINK: "We pray as we live, because we live as we pray." (*CCC 2725)* Is how you're living reflecting how you pray? How should you approach God through your life and your prayer?

DO: What 'road sign' would you add to the prayer roadmap? Write your suggestions all over the page.

BE LITTLE

Be Authentic

BE LOVE

Be Vulnerable

Be True

Be Open

03 Prayer As Devotion

THINK: "If we do not want to act habitually according to the Spirit of Christ, neither can we pray habitually in his name." (*CCC 2725*) Do your habits reflect your closeness to the Lord? Our Catholic faith presents us many gifts to help us to pray and worship our Lord. A few are listed below.

DO: What devotional habits do you have? Circle the ones you practice or would like to practice. If you don't see your habit or don't see the one you'd like to adopt, write it in under each section.

Daily:
- Reading Scripture

Lectio Divina
- Morning Offering Prayer
- 1 Hail Mary, 1 Our Father, (at least)
- Seven Hail Marys for Our Lady's Seven Sorrows
- Angelus
- Liturgy of the Hours
- Rosary
- Divine Mercy Chaplet

Weekly:
- Mass, Sunday & daily Mass
- Abstaining from meat on Fridays, all year
- Adoration Hour

Monthly:
- Sacrament of Reconciliation

Annually:
- Consecrations to Jesus through Mary or St. Joseph

"

God would never inspire me with desires which cannot be realized; so in spite of my littleness, I can hope to be a saint.

St. Therese of Lisieux

"

FOR FUTURE READING:

The Story of a Soul

by St. Therese of Lisieux

Discussion Questions

1. Does knowing that God wants an intimate, loving relationship with you affect how you approach Him?
2. What can you improve in your prayer life? Are there areas you have neglected or areas you'd like to progress into further?
3. How can you and your (future) spouse grow in your relationship with God? How can this trickle into the prayer life of your children (one day)?

Create: Write A Letter

Letter writing is increasingly being pushed aside for the latest technological communications, but there is something inherently human in the creation of letters, words, sentences, paragraphs, and stories. It's personal, and it is *always* appreciated.

INSTRUCTIONS

Take some time now to write a letter to God. What do you want to say to Him, your Father, who made you? The one who yearns for your love and who wants to spend eternity with you. Do you know Him? Are you familiar friends or like distant relatives? Do you return or shun His love? Are you angry or joyful when you hear His name? Do you desire to one day see His face? Pour whatever is on your heart out onto paper remembering that our Creator loves you so much that He brought you forth into existence. As a Father, His mercy and love for **you** is endless.

Dear God

Love,
your beloved daughter

Word of the Day

Take some time and meditate on this word. How would you describe it? What does it mean to you? What do you think of when you hear it? What do you know about it? Categorize your thoughts and feelings about this word in the columns below.

Positives	Negatives

"Because of the grace given me by God to be a minister of Christ Jesus..."
(Romans 15:15-16)

George Washington and Jesus, Coming to Know and Love the Lord!

by Fr. Brett Brannen

Why did God make me? As a child, I memorized the answer to that question in the old Baltimore catechism: "God made me to know him, to love him and to serve him in this life, so that I may be happy with him forever in the next." But how does a person come to really know God? How can I better know Jesus, love him and serve him?

Let's say that I am teaching you a history class on the life of George Washington. I tell the class that they will have to *read two books* about his life, *listen and take notes* in class, and then *write an essay* for their final exam entitled: "I Really Know George Washington." And being the wonderful, conscientious students that you are, you read every page of the two books, really listen in class and study hard. At the end of the semester, do you think you would really know our first president? No. You would know a lot about him, but you would not know him, because you see, he is dead. He lived a long time ago. He is a person and every person is made in the image and likeness of God, with a mind, heart, soul and body. The gifts you have which come with your human soul are memory, intellect, free will and imagination. But since George Washington is dead, since his body and soul are separated, he cannot talk to us and thus we cannot really know him.

But suppose I had the power to raise George Washington from the dead, and every day of the week, he would come to the class and speak with you all for the whole hour. He would tell stories about his life and times, his difficulties, his family, and he would answer your questions about what he thought, felt and did. He would share his memory, intellect, free will and imagination with you.

You would still read the two books, and this information gives you lots of questions to ask him when he comes to class! Now, at the end of the year, **you would really know this man**. You would know about him, having read the history books and listened to him in class, and you would know him; his personality, his laugh, the way he held his eyebrows when he was thinking about your questions, his courage and his goodness.

Coming to truly know and love Jesus follows this same pattern. From your upbringing and education, you may know a lot about Jesus. You may have memorized the Ten Commandments and the Seven Sacraments, the four marks of the Catholic Church and what constitutes mortal and venial sin. You may have studied about Jesus' death and resurrection, and that he has gone to prepare a place for you in Heaven. And you know that Heaven and hell are true. But knowing a lot about Jesus and his teachings does not mean that you really know Him, and His great love for you. This is an acquired, experiential knowledge. This is grace, which opens our eyes to the other.

If you really want to know Jesus, then you will first need to read two books: *God's Word-the Holy Bible*; *and I recommend, the Catechism of the Catholic Church*. You will need to *listen in class (the classroom of prayer), take notes (keep a spiritual journal), ask questions and be patient.* And you will have to *spend this time every day in silent prayer, talking to Jesus and listening to Jesus,* as in the analogy above. Jesus is not dead. He rose from the dead. His human soul and body were separated at death, but they are back together now, joined to his divinity. And He very much wants to talk to you, listen to you and spend time with you.

I know. He is very quiet. When we try to pray, we are often discouraged by this seeming silence. We exasperate: "Jesus does not talk to me!" But if you persevere, putting a daily prayer time on your schedule, you will begin to hear his voice. I promise you this. Ask Jesus questions about what you have read in his Word or in his teachings…and then be quiet and wait for the answer. Ask him another question. "Jesus what do you want me to do about this relationship? Where do you want me to go to college? Please tell me how to be happy!" Wait in silence. Listening is loving!

This personal friendship with the Lord; this intimate relationship of love with Jesus, is the purpose of your life. It will bring you happiness and fulfillment, and it will spare you much pain. There is an old saying that "knowledge maketh a bloody entrance." It means that to really learn something important or to know Someone Important, requires much effort and patience! But it will be worth it. I promise you that Jesus is worth any and all effort!

Why did God make me? God made me to know him, to love him and to serve him in this life, so that I may be happy with him forever in the next.

Section II
Community

Find these paragraphs in the Catechism of the Catholic Church, read along, and listen closely as your facilitator focuses on key points.

Topic	Catechism
1. Mystical Body Of Christ	1. CCC 779, 791, 809
2. Mission	2. CCC 355, 863
3. Communion with Christ	3. CCC 384, 1416
4. Communion of Saints	4. CCC 958
5. Unity	5. CCC 1474, 1477

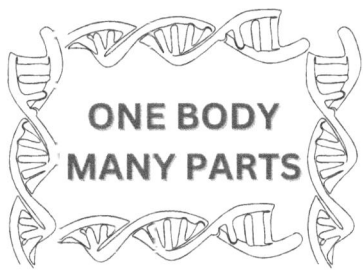

ONE BODY
MANY PARTS

Catechism Notes

Write down your individual notes as you listen to or read along with the Catechism of the Catholic Church.

Mystical Body Of Christ CCC 779, 791, 809

Mission CCC 355, 863

Communion with Christ CCC 384, 1416

Communion of Saints CCC 958

Unity CCC 1474, 1477

02 Interdependence

> For as in one body we have many parts, and all the parts do not have the same function, so we, though many, are one body in Christ and individually parts of one another. Since we have gifts that differ according to the grace given to us, let us exercise them: if prophecy, in proportion to the faith, if ministry, in ministering; if one is a teacher, in teaching; if one exhorts, in exhortation; if one contributes, in generosity; if one is over others, with diligence; if one does acts of mercy, with cheerfulness.
> (Rom 12:4-8)

THINK: We are all called to the mission of **spreading the kingdom**. This starts in the home. This starts in our own families. We are to use our gifts for the good of the whole.

DO: How can you spread the kingdom amongst your family, friends, (future) spouse, and (future) children? List your ideas below.

Family:

Friends:

Spouse:

Children:

03 Friendship

Vulnerability

"Woman naturally seeks to embrace that which is living, personal, and whole. To cherish, guard, protect, nourish and advance growth is her natural, maternal yearning. "

- St. Teresa Benedicta of the Cross

Reciprocity

"I felt more than devotion for her [St. Cecilia]; it was the real tenderness of a friend. She became my saint of predilection, my intimate confidante."

- St. Thérèse of Lisieux

Delight

"God sends us friends in the whirlpool of struggle. In the company of friends, we will find strength to attain our sublime ideal."

-St. Maximilian Kolbe

THINK: Take a few minutes to brainstorm how you can become more vulnerable in your current relationships (with your parents, friends, or romantic relationship), how you can more readily receive friendship and love in these relationships, and how you can delight in your friendship.

DO: Write your thoughts in the columns below.

"

This spiritual love is the kind of love I would desire us to have. Even though in the beginning it is not so perfect, the Lord will gradually perfect it. Let us begin by using the suitable means, for, even though the love bears with it some natural tenderness, no harm will be done provided this tenderness is shown toward all.

St. Teresa of Avila

"

FOR FUTURE READING:

The Interior Castle
by St. Teresa of Avila

Discussion Questions

1. How do I view and treat my family, friends, acquaintances, and enemies as members of Christ's Mystical Body? And those outside His Mystical Body?
2. Where can I grow in my spiritual love of others? How can I honor their unique gifts?
3. St. Clare said, "We become what we love, and who we love shapes what we become." What do you love? Who do you love? How do they shape who you are now? How do you foresee them shaping you in the future?

Create: Crochet a Cross

Handicrafts have been largely discarded as a waste of time or unnecessary in our current day and age. Though you may be able to easily buy quality products at the touch of a button, there is immense value and worth in using your own two hands to create something from seemingly nothing. It takes time, sacrifice, skill, and patience. Sometimes you make mistakes, but those are simply learning lessons gifted to you along the way.

INSTRUCTIONS

Follow the directions & pictures below to create your own cross. Notice how each chain builds upon the next to eventually make something tightly knit and beautiful. You may hit a few snags, but *stay calm* and *persevere*.

Supplies: - yarn (worsted weight) - crochet hook (size H) - scissors

  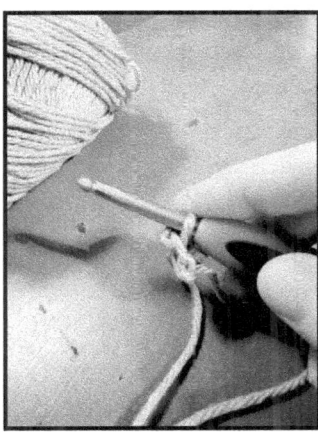

1. Make a slip knot onto the crochet hook.

2. Chain 5. (If you do not know how to do a chain stitch, please find a quick tutorial online.)

3. Take the tail of yarn and pull it through the loop to make a circle.

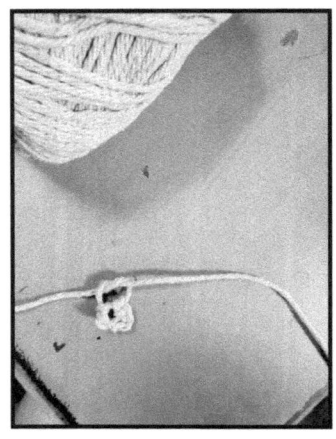

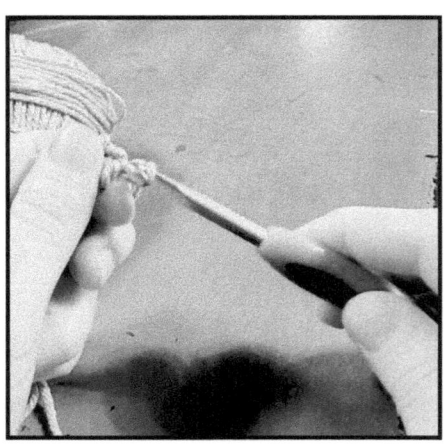

4. Cut your yarn, and tie a simple knot to anchor your circle.

5. Place your hook through the circle, loop the yarn, and pull it through the circle.

6. Pull up a loop.

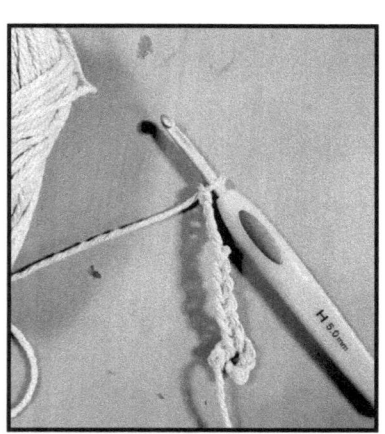

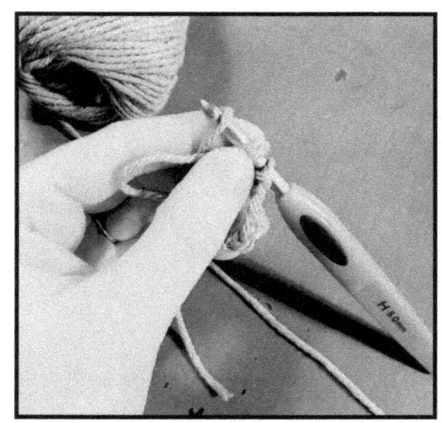

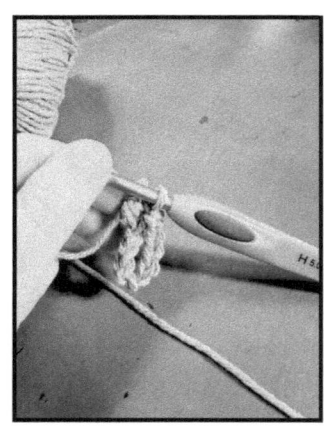

7. Chain 10.

8. On the last stitch, place a slip stitch through the original 5 chain circle.

9. Pull up a loop, and repeat steps 6, 7, & 8 two more times.

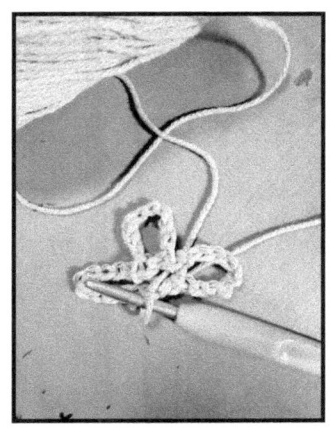 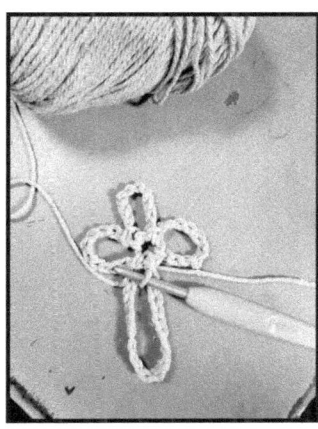 

10. Once you've secured the last chain of 10, pull up a loop, and chain 20.

11. Repeat step 8.

12. Cut away from the roll of yarn.

13. Using the original tail end and end of the yarn, tie it off with a simple knot.

These little crosses make great bookmarks or ornaments. Do you have a certain blanket that is your go-to security blanket? Is it made of yarn? Did someone you know and love make it for you? Have you ever noticed how these blankets are made up of many chains and special knots? If one of the chains is severed, the entire blanket will unravel, but while the chains remain interlocked, there is strength in their connection.

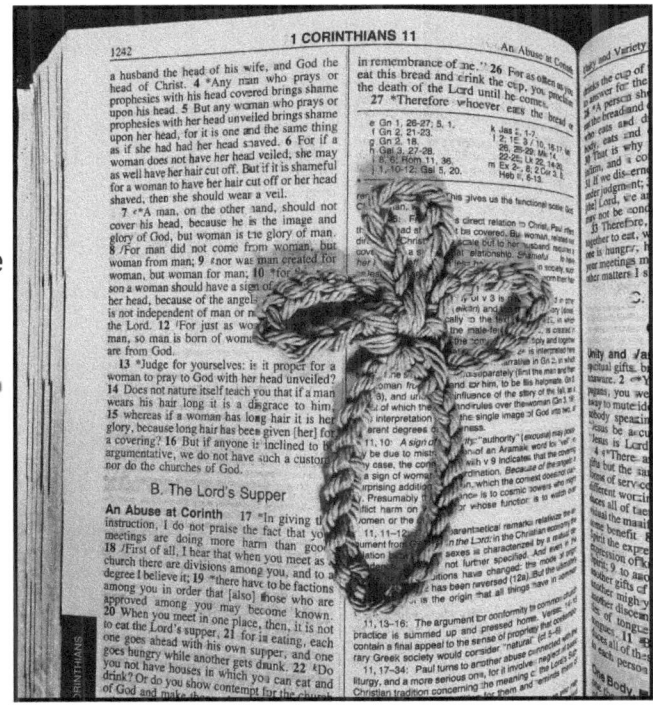

VULNERABLE

Take some time and meditate on this word. How would you describe it? What does it mean to you? What do you think of when you hear it? What do you know about it? Categorize your thoughts and feelings about this word in the columns below.

Positives	Negatives

"Because of the grace given me by God to be a
minister of Christ Jesus…"
(Romans 15:15-16)

The Friends That Make Us

by Fr. Theodore Agba

When I joined the minor seminary at the age of 10, I had two great friends: Lawrence, who was my classmate and Emmanuel, who was a year behind me. I am not sure how my life would have turned out if I didn't have these two in my life, but it is difficult to imagine that life would have been anywhere near as fruitful and rewarding as it has been so far.

We were all united at the minor seminary with a common goal in mind: the hope of one day becoming Catholic priests. Lawrence and Emmanuel were both unique in their own ways and I was drawn to each for different reasons. For sure, they had what I didn't so, I got close to them to be challenged to grow in those areas of my life.

Lawrence was very smart and possessed a wisdom that was far beyond his age, and it was noticeable by many. At the age of 12, he had already started writing a book which he is still working on to this day. He has gone on to write and publish three other books, but the one from 20 years ago is still unfinished. Spending time with him as a young lad, I learned patience and to be more reflective of the choices I was making and how they were affecting me and the people around me. Something that if it was told to me by a priest or teacher at that age, I probably wouldn't have taken it to heart as I did seeing Lawrence truly live it out in his life. This challenged me to begin to see life differently. Emmanuel, on the other hand, was the epitome of holiness for the whole seminary, and we all looked up to him for his exemplary life. He had a great devotion to the Precious Blood of Jesus, so he stayed awake praying in seminary chapel between 11pm to 3am every Thursday.

This was called the Gethsemane Hours. His holiness was contagious enough that many of us started joining him for this Gethsemane Hours. We did this until the rector of the minor seminary had to put an end to it because too many students were sleeping in the classrooms the next day. With Emmanuel, I learned how to pray and surrender everything to God, and trust that He will always watch over me. If someone knew the best way to do something and that something was important to
you, you would do anything to learn from that person. Isn't it? That is what I did by becoming friends with Lawrence and Emmanuel. Through them, I learned from a tender age that the holy life is possible, and I know I am still a work in progress, but these two had a great impact on my life, and I am ever grateful for their friendship that has in many ways made me the man I am today.

Many young people in our secular world cannot make sense of life because the culture of death tries to deprive them of a true relationship with God. Making them feel like a holy and virtuous life is not possible or not important at all. So, each passing day is a frustrating attempt to make sense of life without access to crucial pieces. Having good mentors, teachers, responsible adults, parents, and in my case, good friends can help put the crucial pieces together and reorient our lives toward what matters most, God. The first disciples were just regular people like you and I, who were just going about their regular business with not much purpose or meaning. They were fishermen, tax collectors, traders and zealots, fighting for a cause they knew not its end. Such were their lives until they met a great friend, Jesus of Nazareth, who became everything good to them. A teacher, master, brother, and savior. This encounter with Jesus was a game-changer for them. He filled their lives with a sense of purpose and direction. He taught them that a holy and virtuous life was possible, and they saw him live it out as he ministered to people of all works of life.

Among these band of brothers and friends, he instituted the sacrament of his body and blood, the Eucharist which is the source and summit of the Christian life. He said to them, "Take; this is my body... and he took the cup and when he had given thanks, he gave to them saying, 'This is my blood of the covenant which is poured out for many." Mark 14:22-24. If you knew today was your very last day, how would you spend it? Jesus chose to spend it with his band of friends and to give them the best gift ever, His very Self as food for strength and nourishment that will continue to challenge them to become that which the Lord wants them to be. As they spent time with Jesus and ate and drank of his body and blood, they eventually started becoming like him.
Who are you spending time with and what influence do they have on your life?

When I was in seminary, a retreat facilitator giving a talk on how to be holy, asked us the question: "Who are the five people you spend most time with?" Are they virtuous people? Do they challenge you to be a better person, or do they fuel a certain lifestyle you are working your hardest to get out of? The people we spend the most time with, to a large extent, make us or influence our life choices, and it is very important to be intentional about the friends we keep.

Perhaps, may I suggest that, like the Apostles, we make Jesus a friend by spending some of our time in the day before the Blessed Sacrament. How about 1 hour of your time with the Lord? If this is not possible every day, how about beginning and ending each day in prayer with the Lord. This can be a good place to begin with hope of continued growth in relationship with Jesus.

May I also introduce you to another kind of friends you can make, The Saints. You can find them in the bookshelves of your school library or a click away on your search apps on your smartphones. Read about them and see you growing in love with them and your life-changing for the better. Familiarize yourself with the liturgical calendar and commit to reading about the life of the saint being celebrated for each day. Draw from their virtuous and courageous lives and watch your life become happy and truly fulfilling.

Sacrament of Marriage

01 What Is Marriage?

Find these paragraphs in the Catechism of the Catholic Church, read along, and listen closely as your facilitator focuses on key points.

Topic	Catechism
1. One Flesh	1. CCC 372
2. Symbol of the Church	2. CCC 753, 1617
3. Order of Creation	3. CCC 1603
4. Image of Love of God	4. CCC 1604, 1609
5. Covenant	5. CCC 1612-1614

Covenant

"A solemn promise, fortified by an oath, concerning future action."
- The Catholic Encyclopedia

Catechism Notes

Write down your individual notes as you listen to or read along with the Catechism of the Catholic Church.

One Flesh CCC 372

Symbol of the Church CCC 753, 1617

Order of Creation CCC 1603

Image of Love of God CCC 1604, 1609

Covenant CCC 1612-1615

02 From the Beginning

JESUS SAYS

MATTHEW 19: 3-12

Bible | Scripture | Word of God | 73 Book Canon

Some Pharisees approached him, and tested him, saying, "Is it lawful for a man to divorce his wife for any cause whatever?"

He said in reply, "Have you not read that from the beginning the Creator 'made them male and female' and said, 'For this reason a man shall leave his father and mother and be joined to his wife, and the two shall become one flesh'? So they are no longer two, but **one flesh**. Therefore, **what God has joined together, no human being must separate.**" They said to him, "Then why did Moses command that the man give the woman a bill of divorce and dismiss [her]?"

He said to them, "Because of the hardness of your hearts Moses allowed you to divorce your wives, but from the beginning it was not so.

I say to you, whoever divorces his wife (unless the marriage is unlawful) and marries another commits adultery." [His] disciples said to him, "If that is the case of a man with his wife, it is better not to marry." He answered, "Not all can accept [this] word, but only those to whom that is granted. Some are incapable of marriage because they were born so; some, because they were made so by others; some, because they have renounced marriage for the sake of the kingdom of heaven. Whoever can accept this ought to accept it."

THINK: In John 6:67, Jesus asks His twelve disciples if they also want to leave after a particularly hard teaching. What has happened in your life that challenges Jesus' teaching on marriage and divorce? Do you too want to leave Him?

DO: Take a few minutes to reflect on this scripture passage. Close your eyes and quiet your heart. Imagine yourself there in front of Jesus while He says these words. What is your reaction? Are you fearful? Anxious? Distrustful? Are you at peace? Calm? Grateful? Sit with Jesus in this moment.

03 Wedding Vows

THINK: God's love for us is ALWAYS free, total, faithful, and fruitful. In our (future) spousal relationship, how are we called to practically live out this love freely, totally, faithfully, and fruitfully?

DO: Write your thoughts and ideas on how to do that in the circle below.

Freely
25%

Faithfully
25%

Totally
25%

Fruitfully
25%

"

The sacramental union of the two spouses, sealed in the covenant which they enter into before God, endures and grows stronger as the generations pass. It must become a union in prayer.

St. Pope John Paul II

"

FOR FUTURE READING:

GRATISSIMAM SANE (Letter To Families)

by St. Pope John Paul II

Discussion Questions

1. What qualities do I want my husband to have? Do I currently have some of those same qualities? How can I work on becoming the wife I'd like to be in this current chapter of my life?
2. In what ways (small or large) can I begin practicing self-control and self-denial?
3. Where do I struggle with being a gift and sacrificing my own wants and desires (even if they are good) for the true good of those around me? In what ways can I improve?

Create: Build A House

Marriage is an incredible gift to help us reach holiness and eternity in heaven.
A sacramental marriage is built upon the bedrock of God.

"Everyone who listens to these words of mine and acts on them will be like a wise man who built his house on rock. The rain fell, the floods came, and the winds blew and buffeted the house. But it did not collapse; it had been set solidly on rock. And everyone who listens to these words of mine but does not act on them will be like a fool who built his house on sand. The rain fell, the floods came, and the winds blew and buffeted the house. And it collapsed and was completely ruined." - Matthew 7: 24-27

INSTRUCTIONS

Draw your dream house or build a 3D version with card stock paper. Don't worry if you're "not good" at drawing. Use your imagination. Take some time to really think about not only what it looks like but also who you share it with, what the atmosphere says about you and your desires, and how you and your (future) family will live there. *Follow the steps below for more guidance.*

Supplies: - pencil - pen

1. Sketch your dream home using pencil.

2. Draw all the little details you can think of.

3. Trace your drawing in pen.

Now look at your dream home. Think about how you "built" it, one stroke at a time. Each line created something new. Once it's been traced in pen, it's permanent. There's no erasing what you have built. With Christ as the cornerstone, your (future) marriage and home will be built on a foundation of rock, a foundation that will not collaspe.

MY DREAM HOME

Use this page to draw your dream home.

Word of the Day

SELF-SACRIFICE

Take some time and meditate on this word. How would you describe it? What does it mean to you? What do you think of when you hear it? What do you know about it? Categorize your thoughts and feelings about this word in the columns below.

Positives

Negatives

"Because of the grace given me by God to be a
minister of Christ Jesus..."
(Romans 15:15-16)

Marriage

by Fr. Drew Larkin

Before the serpent in the Garden of Eden, humanity faced his first difficulty. God recognizes that it is not good that Adam is alone. As he names the animals, Adam is searching for someone like himself. After God's creation of Eve from Adam's side, he finally sees her and exclaims, "This one, at last, is bone of my bones and flesh of my flesh." (Gen 2:23) The message is clear; humanity is not just a social being but finds meaning in the other, most especially in the coming together of man and woman. This mystery becomes the foundation for marriage. Marriage begins when a man and woman freely exchange vows with one another. In fact, in the Latin Church, the bride and groom are seen as the ministers of marriage since it is they who offer themselves to one another. Many might see marriage as a social norm that follows a time of successful dating, the "next step," if you will, but with introspection, there is, or, at least, should be, something more going on with a decision to marry. It speaks to the innermost desire of our hearts, our human nature. We desire to be loved and to love. To enter marriage is to experience another committing their life to you no matter what. It is this commitment that we long for, especially in a time when many experience the pain of abandonment and divorce. This commitment, both received and given, provides the structure to have both the bride and groom and their family grow in virtue and in love.

When both know that there is no "escape," it gives the freedom and comfort to love without fear and to know that any problem is something they will have to face together. It corresponds and reminds us of God's love for us, which is unceasing and unconditional. This is why Jesus raises marriage to that of a sacrament because marriage is a sign of God's love and should aspire to the same characteristics of that love, namely that it is freely given (Christ offers Himself by His own will on the Cross), it is total (He holds nothing back from us even to the point of death), it is faithful (unconditional even when we fail Him), and it is fruitful (His sacrifice brings about new life in grace). Thus, marriage lived well becomes an excellent way to prepare for heaven. If I learn what it is to love and be loved and seek to grow in virtue daily, then heaven, which is relationship with the Other, becomes much easier for me to live out.

This may all sound quite idealistic, and indeed it is. This is why in the sacrament of marriage, God gives grace, His real help to husbands and wives to assist them in living out their vocation of marriage. It should also be clear that sacrifice was a vital component of Jesus' love for us. Marriage is no different. If done correctly, marriage should be at odds with our own selfishness and pride. Entering a marriage is not just expanding my concern for myself to one more person but involves a dying to self.

As a bride, you are called to take on the wellbeing of your husband. Can you live for him and his true good? And can you entrust your wellbeing over to him and his concern? Do you trust that he will live for you and your true good? This is the ideal of marriage that again, captures something of the image of God. God is Trinity where the Father empties Himself into the Son and the Son into the Father, a love that is the Holy Spirit.

This self-emptying is the model for true love and for marriage. In God, we also gain a better understanding as to what it means to authentically love someone.

"Love" has many connotations and meanings in our language and it can sometimes become diluted when we apply it to marriage. It is more than feeling an affection for another although this certainly assists us in loving them. It is to will, to choose the good of the other. It is a real choice that I make to love rather than a fleeting feeling that comes and goes with time. Arguably, love is most concrete in marriage in those times when it is more difficult to love. We see this in God's love with his love for humanity in accepting death on the Cross or in examples like the parable of the Prodigal Son which highlights the incredible love and mercy of the father. In the same parable, we see that the love between father and son is not something confined to the two men alone but overflows into a celebration of the community. In the same way marital love, like God's love is diffusive, it can manifest in the presence of children as a result of that love. The fact that God is Love spills over into the creation of humanity. Our origin and existence find their answer in nothing but God's willing choice of our good. In the same way, God intends that children experience something similar concretely in the love of their parents. Even beyond our own family, marriage becomes a reminder to the whole world of our purpose in this world, to love and be loved, and models for all an image of the God who fulfills this most perfectly as we see the characteristics of His love reflected in marriage.

Section IV
Redemptive Suffering

01 What is Redemptive Suffering?

Find these paragraphs in the Catechism of the Catholic Church, read along, and listen closely as your facilitator focuses on key points.

Topic	Catechism
1. Share In Christ's Suffering	1. CCC 428
2. Mystery of Redemption	2. CCC 517
3. Participation In Christ's Suffering	3. CCC 618
4. Take Up One's Cross	4. CCC 1435
5. Grace Is Sufficient	5. CCC 1508
6. Thanksgiving	6. CCC 2648

Now I rejoice in my sufferings for your sake, and in my flesh I am filling up what is lacking in the afflictions of Christ on behalf of his body, which is the church.

Colossians 1:24

Catechism Notes

Write down your individual notes as you listen to or read along with the Catechism of the Catholic Church.

Share In Christ's Suffering CCC 428

Mystery of Redemption CCC 517

Participation In Christ's Suffering CCC 618

Take Up One's Cross CCC 1435

Grace Is Sufficient CCC 1508

Thanksgiving CCC 2648

02 The Beauty of Suffering

Down:

2. an offering
3. a moral virtue whereby a sinner detests his or her sin as an offense against God and resolves to make amends.

Across:

1. abstinence from food and an act of temperance.
4. a conversation, offering, praise, and/or worship with, to, and for the Lord.
5. the third and greatest of the Divine virtues as told by St. Paul (1 Corinthians 13:13); also called charity

03 Offer It Up

THINK: Nobody *wants* to suffer, but regardless of our fears of suffering, suffering is a part of our life here on earth. It is unavoidable, but it is not in vain. We are united to Christ in our joys *and* our sufferings. It is through Him that our suffering has meaning. A common phrase in Catholicism is "to offer it up." We can offer up our biggest sufferings down to our smallest sufferings, knowing that through this mystery, God will use them for His greater glory.

DO: Offer Him your sufferings today. Jot those sufferings down somewhere on this page. Then, envision yourself placing them at the foot of the crucifix while you gaze upon Christ's sacrifice given up for you. Hand over your sufferings to our Lord. Though we may not always see the end results in this life, we have confidence that He turns everything to good, even our suffering.

redemptive suffering is...

- ✓ an act of love
- ✓ sanctifying
- ✓ an act of spiritual communion

And the Lord said to me, "My child, you please Me most by suffering. In your physical as well as your mental sufferings, My daughter, do not seek sympathy from creatures. I want the fragrance of your suffering to be pure and unadulterated. I want you to detach yourself, not only from creatures, but also from yourself…The more you will come to love suffering, My daughter, the purer your love for Me will be".

Saint Maria Faustina Kowalska

FOR FUTURE READING:

Diary of Saint Maria Faustina Kowalska:
Divine Mercy in My Soul
by St. Maria Faustina Kowalska

Discussion Questions

1. Redemptive suffering is one of the hardest teachings of our Lord Jesus Christ. Why do you think He had to suffer for our sins and salvation? What is the significance of His sacrificial love?

2. In today's world, when suffering is perceived as something to be avoided at all costs, how can we "suffer" for Christ in an ordered way? What habits can we form to help us take up our cross?

3. What small things can you offer up? How do you think this notion of "offering it up" can and will affect your life?

Create: Budgeting

Budgeting is a task that we all must tackle at some point in our lives. It takes discipline, self-awareness, and often, self-denial and sacrifice. It's not always a fun task, but it's a skill worth having and doing well.

INSTRUCTIONS

Create a budget. Below are your estimated salary, taxes, and expenses. Factor everything into your budget. Where can you cut costs to have a larger surplus?

Gross Income/Salary: $50,000/year

Taxes: 22%

Net Income (income after taxes):_____

Monthly Income:_____

<u>(% of your net salary)</u>

- Mortgage/Rent: 25%/monthly
- Savings: 10%/monthly
- Car: 10%/monthly
- House & Auto Insurance: 6%/monthly
- Health Insurance: 9%/monthly
- Groceries/Food: 15%/monthly
- Utilites: 12%/monthly
- Miscellaneous: 5%/monthly
- Emergency Fund: 7%/monthly

Monthly Budget

Bills	Cost

Total Cost:

Total Surplus:

Take some time and meditate on this word. How would you describe it? What does it mean to you? What do you think of when you hear it? What do you know about it? Categorize your thoughts and feelings about this word in the columns below.

Positives

Negatives

"Because of the grace given me by God to be a minister of Christ Jesus..."
(Romans 15:15-16)

Redemptive Suffering
by Fr. Daniel Firmin

To live is to suffer. To love is to suffer. How I bear suffering comes from faith in Jesus Christ and the hope that lives within me because of that faith.

I do not know how someone without faith survives suffering. For those who believe in Jesus, follow Him, and claim Him as Lord of our lives, suffering is not only bearable, but can be redemptive – meaning that suffering can contribute to our own redemption and the redemption of others.

Our Savior, through His suffering, redeemed us from our sins and opened our way to eternal happiness, love, and life.

My suffering, because I am a member of the Body of Christ through baptism, contributes to my redemption and holiness and the redemption and holiness of others.

This reality, therefore, helps me maintain joy and a positive attitude when I suffer through my cancer treatments and its effects.

Emotional & Spiritual Intimacy

01 What is Intimacy?

Find these paragraphs in the Catechism of the Catholic Church, read along, and listen closely as your facilitator focuses on key points.

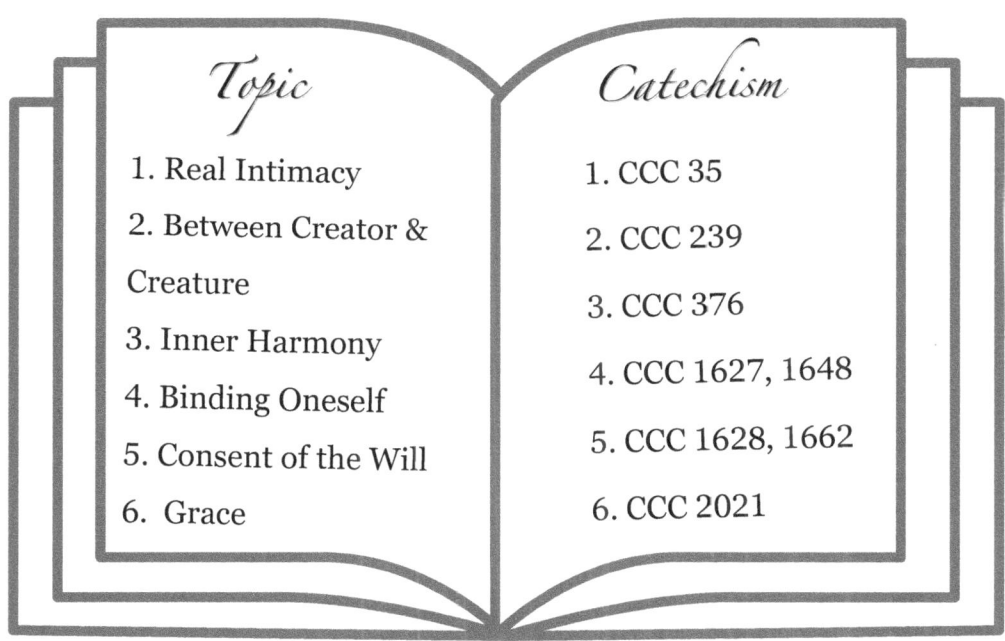

Topic	Catechism
1. Real Intimacy	1. CCC 35
2. Between Creator & Creature	2. CCC 239
3. Inner Harmony	3. CCC 376
4. Binding Oneself	4. CCC 1627, 1648
5. Consent of the Will	5. CCC 1628, 1662
6. Grace	6. CCC 2021

> 🔍 **sainthood**   ×
>
> So be perfect, just as your heavenly Father is perfect.
>
> *Matthew 5:48*

Catechism Notes

Write down your individual notes as you listen to or read along with the Catechism of the Catholic Church.

Real Intimacy CCC 35

Between Creator & Creature CCC 239

Inner Harmony CCC 376

Bind Oneself CCC 1627, 1648

Consent of the Will CCC 1628, 1662

Grace CCC 2021

02 Types of Love

THINK: In our language, the word "love" means many different things. You *love* your new car, you *love* going to the beach, and you *love* your parents. The Ancient Greeks used four words to describe certain types of love.

DO: Next to the arrows below, write some examples of each type of love. They can be examples from your current life or those you hope to be in your future. *Note: Some examples apply to multiple types of love.*

03 Help Get Your Husband To Heaven

RELISH
UNITE
SEE
FIND
ACCEPT
RECEIVE
TRUST
SHED
OPEN

THINK: It may seem daunting, but helping your spouse reach heaven is the divine call for every husband and wife. Your vocation is your journey to sanctity. Through the Sacrament of Marriage, you receive special graces to do this. Listen as your facilitator reads you some ideas on how to do this.

DO: On or around the steps above, jot down your notes from the read-aloud (found on the next page). Write in some practical ways you can help your (future) spouse get to heaven. Be specific.

03 Help Get Your Husband To Heaven

- Read along as your facilitator reads the following.

    - **Open** yourself up to love. How? By doing nothing out of selfishness or vainglory. (see Phil 2:3).
    - **Shed** the desire for self-protection. Strive to be whole and authentic.
    - **Trust** in the Lord that He will provide and will help you & your (future) spouse grow in virtue.
    - **Receive** the fruits of love and then turn and give them away out of love. Jesus asked Bartimeus, "What do you want me to do for you?" (see Mark 10:51). How do you respond to Jesus' question?
    - **Accept** the graces the Lord wants to bestow upon you both through your relationship.
    - **Find** enjoyment in loving God through another.
    - **See** your spouse as someone whom Christ offered himself as sacrifice for.
    - **Unite** yourself to him through Christ's love.
    - **Relish** in doing the will of God with your spouse in fellowship.

- Visualize marriage as a daily climb towards holiness together with your (future) spouse.
- Remember that God designed both male and female and marriage in this manner for a reason.

> Love is indeed "ecstasy," not in the sense of a moment of intoxication, but rather as a journey, an ongoing exodus out of the closed inward-looking self toward its liberation through self-giving, and thus toward authentic self-discovery and indeed the discovery of God: "Whoever seeks to gain his life will lose it, but whoever loses his life will preserve it" (Luke 17:33).

Pope Benedict XVI

FOR FUTURE READING:

DEUS CARITAS EST (God Is Love)
by Pope Benedict XVI

Discussion Questions

1. In what ways does our culture's idea of love and intimacy differ from God's definition of love and intimacy?
2. How can you apply God's love (willing the true good of the other) to your everyday relationship(s)?
3. What are some *healthy* ways of "losing" your life for the sake of others? For the sake of your (future) spouse? For the sake of sanctity?

Create: A Weekly Menu

Everyone has to eat! Being able to provide your (future) spouse and children with a wholesome meal made with love is a tremendous gift. When creating your menu, be mindful of nutrition and your body's needs. *Example: a traditional approach to dinner meals is one meat, one veggie side, and one starch.*

INSTRUCTIONS

Pretend you're cooking for your (future) spouse and family from scratch. Lay out your menu, on the next page, and then list all of the ingredients you will need below. Don't forget simple things such as butter and salt!

☐ _____   ☐ _____

☐ _____   ☐ _____

☐ _____   ☐ _____

☐ _____   ☐ _____

☐ _____   ☐ _____

☐ _____   ☐ _____

☐ _____   ☐ _____

DINNER menu

M

T

W

T

F

S

S

Take some time and meditate on this word. How would you describe it? What does it mean to you? What do you think of when you hear it? What do you know about it? Categorize your thoughts and feelings about this word in the columns below.

Positives   Negatives

"Because of the grace given me by God to be a minister of Christ Jesus…"
(Romans 15:15-16)

Spiritual / Emotional Intimacy
by Fr. Barnabas O'Reilly, O.S.B.

I'll never forget the day I left for the monastery. I had successfully distracted myself from thinking too much about this great leap of faith toward becoming a monk by busying myself with work, setting up goodbye meetings with old friends, attempting to pay off some bills, and trying to figure out which kind of sandals (aka monk slides) I should get before entering.

The day finally came when I had to report to the monastery. I was to arrive before evening prayer, and of course I was running late, sending my last emails before I was away from the internet for a year. In a hurry, I grabbed my two bags and told my parents I was ready to hit the road. As I rushed out of the house, I felt a tap on my shoulder. I turned around and saw my younger brother looking at me. He was only a few years younger than me, and we had been best friends growing up. It hit me all of a sudden that I had forgotten to say goodbye to him, and he was making sure to see me before I left. Quickly, I realized that "seeing me" was all he could do. I saw tears welling up in his eyes, and I saw that he wasn't able to speak. Of course, I started getting emotional too, but I successfully choked down my tears so I could blurt out a very quick and "manly" goodbye. As I walked away from him, I was struck by a deep clarity. I asked myself internally, "Why have I been focused on so many things and people that don't matter?" and furthermore, "Why didn't I spend these past days and weeks spending quality time with my brother?". I knew he was moving toward getting engaged, and I was going off to a monastery, not summer camp. It struck me deeply that while I would see him again, I said goodbye to a certain kind of childhood relationship that we had.

I am sharing this story because it was a moment in which I realized the emotional and spiritual bond between my brother and me was much deeper than I knew. I realized that it is the people that we love the most that we take for granted the most until it hits us suddenly.

I think it would help married couples and those seeking marriage to understand the different definitions of love, according to Aristotle. Most married couples would acknowledge that they share a love of "eros," especially in the beginning. This kind of love is based on attraction and affection for the spouse. Yet if the love does not grow deeper, this "eros" waxes and wanes. This "eros" must also grow into "phila." This is the kind of love Aristotle would describe as "brotherly love" which can be applied to spouses as becoming deep friends beyond simple attraction. Yet even this kind of love can grow deeper to a kind of love that the human heart is truly looking for. This kind of love Aristotle would call "agape", namely unconditional love.

We must be aware of the emotional and spiritual bonds that are created with those around us. Firstly, because as the old adage goes, it is important to "guard your heart" from romantic relationships that really have no potential to grow deeper. What I mean by this is that it is easy for the attraction or "eros" love to cloud one's vision and clarity about whether someone has potential to be a lifelong friend and spouse. Secondly, it is also important to take time away from the distractions of life to recognize the emotional and spiritual love that has formed with our deepest friendships, especially between married couples. Yet I would add that one's emotional love with their spouse will never grow to the great depths possible unless they discover Jesus Christ as the glue that holds their bond together and calls them to ever deeper intimacy with him. Couples that share the commonality of loving Christ and seeking friendship with him open up new horizons for their own friendship in marriage and intimacy because their relationship is built on the foundation of Jesus who is the author of love.

Section VI
Physical Intimacy

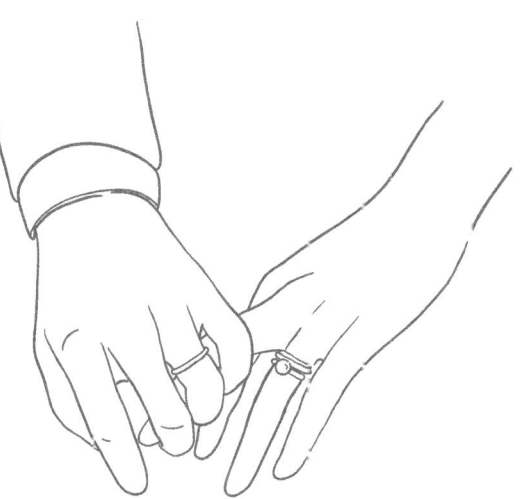

01 What is Physical Intimacy?

Find these paragraphs in the Catechism of the Catholic Church, read along, and listen closely as your facilitator focuses on key points.

Topic	Catechism
1. Sexuality	1. CCC 2360
2. Commitment	2. CCC 2361
3. Joy & Pleasure	3. CCC 2362
4. Union	4. CCC 2363
5. Conjugal Fidelity	5. CCC 2364
6. Fecundity	6. CCC 2366

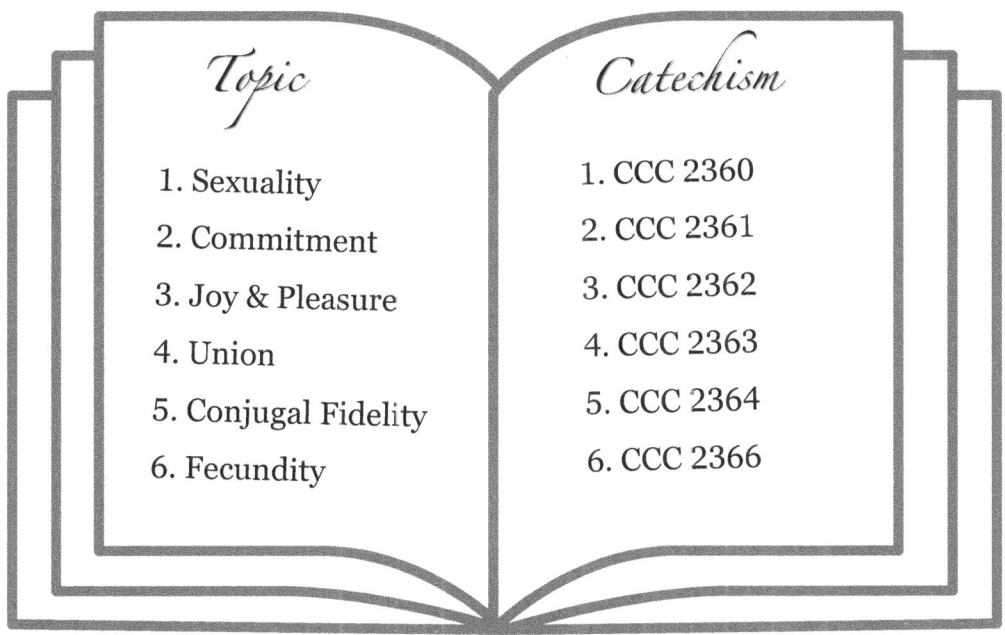

Body + Soul = human

Catechism Notes

Write down your individual notes as you listen to or read along with the Catechism of the Catholic Church.

Sexuality CCC 2360

Commitment CCC 2361

Joy & Pleasure CCC 2362

Union CCC 2363

Conjugal Fidelity CCC 2364

Fecundity CCC 2366

02 Conjugal Love

```
N N H V M S H G D W P P M G B E U A R M V D F U F B Z P N G
O H L S D Q I L C T I W O I I J N L G B J T B A Q C Z Q A Q
F F B V V W C J P U N C Z T Z F M U P U Z O E E P U U L O P
X D K M I V F C T K D C Q T R E C C M W Z P B U E N Y J V E
U A O B N A F G F C I W Y F Y S V S I L M A S N O I S N Q K
U H U L C K J A L M V O F O I I M M O R F W K I M T T Y D N
Z V R L B F N D J N E W Q B S Y W W O Y W G H Q S I I J O P
E U S R G X J R P W L Y W B A L G F M X T E W U B V W W M Y
S X I E D X K Q S H F A P D L R O T H Y S Z W E S E O N Z A
E E A F M O M L J R E N E W A L O F V O W S K E L Y S Q M D
T W L U M K X J A M L P H U F A Q V S O J M N X C S J N Q W
U Y K F O R V A R U J Y R L N L O S P V X Z Y P V N Q P T Y
T O A H G D C S L T P D R W T O V V R P R O C R E A T I V E
F Y G Q P I M Q I U S L U N X V H D S F P F J E K V Q X J N
W T L E D U V W Y A K S G M K E K M E P N U L S G D A S V S
V B Z B O K R I E L F V B P J I J J J B Z T C S K K R R N Q
R H G E K S C V N A X S R C X B L P G V U Y G I X Q N I T V
B N D Q H T X Q U G M C N G E C X B L M S G S O M H D L S O
S P Y G Z S P I R I T U A L C O M M U N I O N N V Q L I B Q
J V Y N V U T R V A M X T X X Z D T D N A A E O N J S U J A
F E D I A A D C D G Y C L Y K N G M I D W U A F L R A N X E
G D J Q E K K E S C U G N E C T N G I J I L D M S G K Y G J
N D I V P E I W T X W P Y P F I S B G D B G H A G R I P H E
T C B D V K G X E X C S B B R B M V K W O T C R A S D H M W
A N G W H N D A J R C W T D A W J N V M H U W R D C E P I H
O O P T K S W G T J A B M M Y I L J W K N W O I L R Y Y B Y
S N Y J V N V F O U F E S M F Z P F S V W H O A M O R P P M
J F H M S Y N K F X V O Y V Y W T C K T D C E G W E L A E P
W E O I E E P C X J E R J W C S Q Z S M Z I G E G W H V B R
F E O A U U B D X F J Q Y E I R C I J F X U E T Y T K L T R
```

Find & circle or highlight the hidden words and phrases.
(hint: only one word is diagonal)

- Love
- Unitive
- Renewal of Vows
- Procreative
- Self Giving
- Spiritual Communion
- Mutual
- Unique Expression of Marriage

03 Be Fruitful And Multiply

THINK: The sexual act within marriage is a total giving of oneself. Conjugal love is an expression of true, self-giving love within the communion of marriage.

DO: Slowly read the statement by Pope St. John Paul II below. Underline and ponder the words that jump out at you.

In his encyclical, *Evangelium Vitae*, Pope St. John Paul II said...

"Even in the midst of difficulties and uncertainties, every person sincerely open to truth and goodness can, by the light of reason and the hidden action of grace, come to recognize in the natural law written in the heart (cf. Rom 2:14-15) the sacred value of human life from its very beginning until its end, and can affirm the right of every human being to have this primary good respected to the highest degree."

It takes three to make love, not two: you, your spouse, and God. Without God people only succeed in bringing out the worst in one another. Lovers who have nothing else to do but love each other soon find there is nothing else. Without a central loyalty, life is unfinished.

Venerable Fulton Sheen

FOR FUTURE READING:

Three to Get Married

by Venerable Fulton Sheen

Discussion Questions

1. Knowing that the purpose of the sexual act is both unitive and procreative, what are some of the other fruits of conjugal love? (ex. pleasure, connection, intimacy, etc.)
2. How can you embrace how God made you (body *and* soul) at this stage in your life?
3. Understanding that children are a gift, not a right, what about having children makes you the most nervous? The most excited?

Create: A Watercolor Painting 06

Painting is a form of creativity that many are intimidated by, but when you were a child, you weren't scared to paint. You enjoyed the messiness and the process. You enjoyed the act of creating. Enjoy it again now.

INSTRUCTIONS

Use watercolors to paint the background of your paper. Once dry, take a marker, and write the scripture passage below. Follow the steps below for more guidance.

Supplies: - thick paper - watercolor paints - paintbrush - water - marker

And the two shall become one flesh.

MARK 10:8

1. Gather your supplies & wet your brush in the water.

2. Dip your brush into whatever color you'd like and paint the color onto the page. Clean your brush in the water before each color change.

3. Paint as much or as little of the page as you'd like. Try not to think too much as you blend.

4. When you are finished, clean your brush and let the paper dry.

5. Then use the marker to write the scripture verse in whatever style you would like.

Consider getting a frame for your artwork or simply displaying it in a place where you can ponder its meaning as you go about your life.

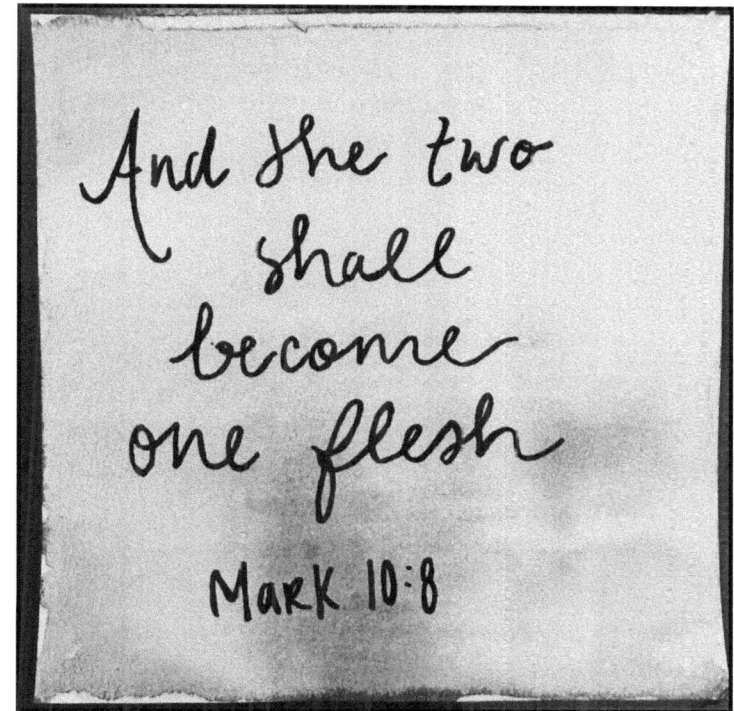

And the two shall become one flesh

Mark 10:8

Take some time and meditate on this word. How would you describe it? What does it mean to you? What do you think of when you hear it? What do you know about it? Categorize your thoughts and feelings about this word in the columns below.

Positives | Negatives

"Because of the grace given me by God to be a minister of Christ Jesus…"
(Romans 15:15-16)

Physical Intimacy
by Fr. Gregory Visca, O.S.B.

In 2009, James Cameron came out with the movie *Avatar*. The two protagonists, Sully and Niytiri, form a romantic relationship as literally star-crossed lovers. There's a line of dialogue that really stood out to me as I watched it. It was the way that the Na'vi, the blue characters, greeted each other by saying, "I see you."

This isn't some insignificant superficial way of saying hello but a way of greeting that sees into the depths of the other person. When we speak of sexual intimacy, it goes beyond just physical touch but seeing the entire person with all their vulnerabilities, with all their scars and blemishes, with all their weaknesses on full display.

Intimacy involves being vulnerable to another person. In the sexual act, the spouses are giving themselves entirely over to the other in their minds, in their hearts, and in their bodies. It is more or less a commonly known fact that 90% of our language is actually body language. What we say in the marital bed is an echo of what is expressed at the altar.

So, when two become one flesh, they're saying to each other in sickness and in health, in riches and poor for the entirety of this life, I am yours, and you are mine. This intimacy only increases over time. We might get discouraged when we look at our own bodies and wonder how could the other love me as the "dad body" sets in or the stretch marks from having kids come, but it is in those things that the other can cherish all the more. It is a reality of a life shared together through many trials and joys that only adds to the experience of coming together in a sexually intimate way.

Motherhood

01 What is Motherhood?

Find these paragraphs in the Catechism of the Catholic Church, read along, and listen closely as your facilitator focuses on key points.

Topic	Catechism
1. God's Tenderness	1. CCC 239
2. Nurturers	2. CCC 1251
3. Safeguard Grace	3. CCC 1255
4. Heralds of Faith	4. CCC 1656
5. Initiation Into Life	5. CCC 2207
6. Fecundity	6. CCC 2398

Catechism Notes

Write down your individual notes as you listen to or read along with the Catechism of the Catholic Church.

God's Tenderness CCC 239

Nurturers CCC 1251

Safeguard Grace CCC 1255

Heralds of Faith CCC 1656

Initiation Into Life CCC 2207

Fecundity CCC 2398

02 What It Means to Be 'Mother'?

Her children rise up and call her blessed

Proverbs 31:28

THINK: Read Proverbs 31:10-31. The Valiant Woman reflects lasting beauty and charm. Through use of her talents in fear and love of the Lord, she is praised. Motherhood is made up of countless small acts of love.

DO: List five more talents a wife and mother should possess to give glory to God in her everyday life.

1 RESOURCEFUL .... 1 ....

2 SKILLFUL .... 2 ....

3 THOUGHTFUL .... 3 ....

4 COMPASSIONATE .... 4 ....

5 WISE .... 5 ....

03 Growth In Virtue

THINK: Children are **gifts** from God. It is a mother's responsibility to nurture and nourish her children, but they are not ours to keep. We are to be stewards of God's love for them on their own journey to heaven. We do this by helping them to become virtuous.

DO: How can you teach your (future) children the virtues? Write your ideas along the chart.

> # To be a mother is to nourish and protect true humanity and bring it to development.

St. Teresa Benedicta of the Cross

FOR FUTURE READING:

Essays on Woman

by Edith Stein (St. Teresa Benedicta of the Cross)

Discussion Questions

1. Motherhood is a noble calling. It is a calling that, in some way, all women are called to fulfill, even if not solely through biological children. Besides your own mother, who has mothered you in your life?

2. We all have ideas of perfection and fears of not attaining that perfection, especially when it comes to the type of mother we'd like to be. In what ways can we emulate Our Lady, the perfect mother, in our (future) motherhood?

3. Knowing that children are gifts, *not burdens or accessories,* how can you guide your (future) child(ren) in their path to heaven?

Create: Embroider

Embroidery is like painting with thread, and it's much easier than you'd think. Women have been embroidering since the 3rd century B.C. to adorn clothes, keep track of linens, and for artistry. It was a skill that was passed down from mother to daughter for generations. Think of these women through the centuries as you use needle and thread to create something out of seemingly nothing.

INSTRUCTIONS

Follow the steps to create your own unique embroidered work of art.

Supplies: - Miraculous Medal - embroidery needle - embroidery thread - small embroidery hoop - scissors - pencil or fabric marker - small piece of plain fabric

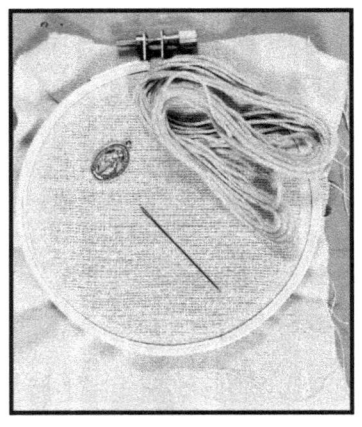
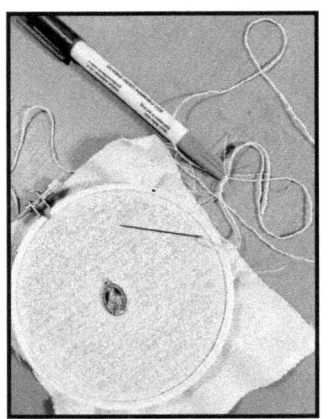
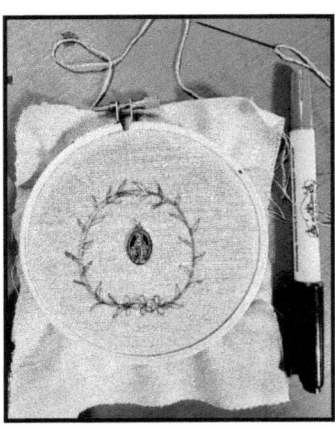

1. Place your fabric into your hoop, making sure it is taut. Cut an arm length piece of thread. Then split your thread in half by pulling three strands apart from the cut piece of thread.

2. Thread your needle and knot the end. Then sew the Miraculous medal where you would like it on the hoop. Come from back to front with your needle at least two times through the medal's clasp circle.

3. Use a pencil or fabric marker to draw a design around the medal.

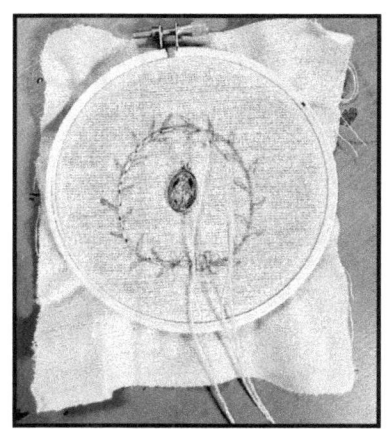 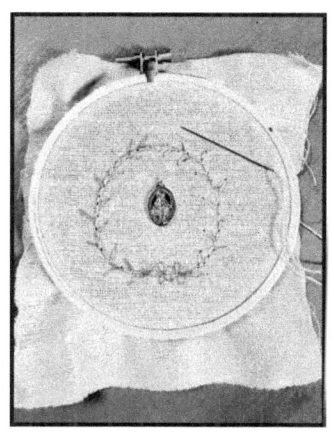 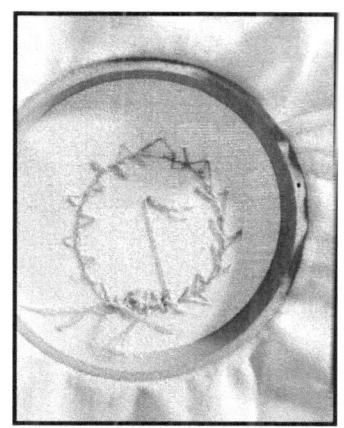

4. Pull your needle from back to front and vice versa along the lines you've drawn.

5. Your stitches can be as simple or as complicated as you'd like to follow your pattern.

6. Tie off the last stitch with a simple knot, and cut the excess thread.

Leave the fabric on the hoop and glue the fabric's edges to the back for a pretty ornament or wall hanging or place your art into a special frame.

Word of the Day

Take some time and meditate on this word. How would you describe it? What does it mean to you? What do you think of when you hear it? What do you know about it? Categorize your thoughts and feelings about this word in the columns below.

Positives	Negatives

"Because of the grace given me by God to be a
minister of Christ Jesus..."
(Romans 15:15-16)

<u>Motherhood</u>
by Fr. Joachim Morgan, O.S.B

I think it is fair to say that all women will live some aspect of motherhood. To understand that there is biological motherhood, but there is also spiritual, I want to briefly focus on the Blessed Mother and how mothers take a role in a priest's life.

From the moment the Archangel Gabriel approached the Blessed Mother and she gave her yes, she became a biological mother. The Word of God became Flesh in her very womb. She carried the God-Man for nine months and brought Him into the world. We see how she cared and watched Him as shepherds came to adore, Magi brought gifts, He was presented in the Temple, the Holy Family fled to Egypt, then back to Nazareth, and even lost Him for three days. We see her motherly heart pierced with sorrow. In the brief accounts of Christ's early life, we get a glimpse of Mary as mother. We know she swaddled Him to keep Him warm, nursed Him so He was fed, and made sure that religious observations were taken care of as well. The Blessed Mother took care of her only Son physically, spiritually, and emotionally.

When Christ set out for His public ministry, I can't help but wonder how the Blessed Mother felt. Jesus is baptized, goes into the desert, and is tempted by Satan. His first miracle comes about by her asking, but she will witness that not all of His moments are water to wine—He will be mocked, people will doubt Him, people will start to plan to have Him killed—and she patiently stands around in the background, not drawing attention to herself. Then Christ is arrested, found guilty, and sentenced to crucifixion.

As she sees her Son, hanging upon the Cross, He calls out to her, "Woman, behold your Son." She must have felt every scourge that had fallen upon the flesh of her flesh, the bone of her bone. She felt the wounds her in hands and feet. She who will be crowned with stars must have felt every thorn that pierced her beloved Son's head.

As she looks upon Him with wonder, sorrow, and love, she hears Him speak to the Beloved Disciple, "Behold, your mother." And the Beloved Disciple takes the Blessed Mother into his life that very moment. She then sees her Son breathe His last and have His side and Heart pierced, and her heart is pierced as well. This whole afternoon brings about our redemption and also gives us Mary as our mother. The one who carried the One whom the heavens could not contain, the one who gave Him life, the one who nourished Him, the one who cleaned Him, the one who asked for His first miracle, is now our mother as well. She gives us beautiful advice, her last recorded words, "Do whatever He tells you."

For mothers of priests, there is a beautiful tradition that speaks a lot. When a priest is getting ordained, his hands are tied up with a piece of cloth to show he is not yet a priest. His hands are eventually freed and anointed, and with that same cloth, his hands are wiped of the anointing oil. As a newly ordained priest, he then presents this cloth to his mother. When she finishes her earthly race, she will be buried with this cloth so that when she is brought before God and asked, "What have you done?" She can answer, "I have given you my son as a priest." This cloth is a reminder to the priest of the care his mother showed him in his life—the cleaning, bathing, feeding, and rocking to sleep, and all the other little acts of love a mother showers upon her children.

Again, I said that all women are called to motherhood. There is a feminine spirituality that shows care, nourishment, and concern that is unique and amazing. As St Teresa Benedicta of the Cross said, "The children in school . . . do not need merely what we have, but rather what we are." (*Essays on Women*). Women are created with a specific place to allow a baby to grow. They are made to receive life itself. I see that with the Blessed Mother, my own mom, and women that I encounter.

Section VIII
Summary

Find these paragraphs in the Catechism of the Catholic Church, read along, and listen closely as your facilitator focuses on key points.

Topic	Catechism
1. Seek God	1. CCC 30, 2726
2. Love God	2. CCC 358, 575, 1033, 1728, 1844, 2093
3. Trust God	3. CCC 27, 150, 154, 215, 227, 304
4. Surrender to God	4. CCC 931, 945, 1078, 2712, 2825

Catechism Notes

Write down your individual notes as you listen to or read along with the Catechism of the Catholic Church.

Seek God CCC 30, 2726

Love God CCC 358, 575, 1033, 1728, 1844, 2093

Trust God CCC 27, 150, 154, 215, 227, 304

Surrender to God CCC 931, 945, 1078, 2712, 2825

02 What Is Love?

"Whoever is without love does not know God, for God is love."

"My soul proclaims the greatness of the Lord."

"The fear of God prepares a place for love."

"We become what we love and who we love shapes what we become."

"Do even the smallest things out of great love."

"Love is always only 'becoming.'"

"To love is to will the good of the other."

"Love is shown more in deeds than in words."

THINK: Christ, the Blessed Mother, and all of the angels and Saints show us the meaning of love. What stories come to mind when you think of the meaning of love? They can be from your own life, scripture, or saint stories.

DO: Circle your favorite quote above. Take a guess at who said it. Then, ponder and pray with the quote. What is God trying to show you through these words?

1. St. Thomas Aquinas, Summa Theologica
2. St. Augustine, Ninth Homily on 1 John, 4
3. St. Ignatius of Loyola
4. Our Blessed Mother, Luke 1: 46
5. John 4:8
6. Pope St. John Paul II
7. St. Clare of Assisi
8. St. Faustina

03 Trust & Surrender

THINK: Jesus said, ""I am the way and the truth and the life. No one comes to the Father except through me." (John 14:6.) Close your eyes, and let His words sink into your soul.

DO: In what ways can you trust God more *today*? In what ways can you surrender to Him? Fill the stars with your answers.

LET US PRAY

Lord, please give me the grace to trust you and to surrender everything to you. Jesus, I trust in you. Jesus, I surrender myself to You.
Amen.

Pray, hope, and don't worry.

St. Padre Pio

FOR FUTURE READING:

Trustful Surrender to Divine Providence: The Secret of Peace and Happiness by St. Claude de la Colombière & Fr. Jean Baptiste Saint-Jure

Discussion Questions 05

1. Why should you seek to know and love God? How can you seek God in your daily life while in this current chapter?
2. Knowing that God is love, what does that mean for you and your relationships?
3. What are some practical ways to let go of any fear or anxiety you may feel? How can you open yourself up to experience peace through God's love for you? In what ways can surrendering to God's will for you replace any despair you may feel with gratitude?

Create: Sewing A Button

In a fast-moving world, our culture tends to throw away the old to make way for the new without much thought for mending. In the past, mending was a necessary skill to continue the life of clothing and make good use of the resources at hand. When a dress or shirt loses one its buttons, it's not trash. It's an easy and satisfying fix.

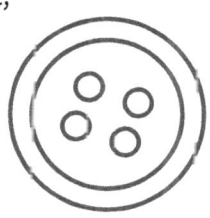

INSTRUCTIONS

Follow the steps to learn how to sew a button onto fabric.

Supplies: - a scrap piece of fabric - 1 button - a needle (you can use the same embroidery needle from your last project) - thread (you can also use the same thread from the last project, but only use one strand) - scissors

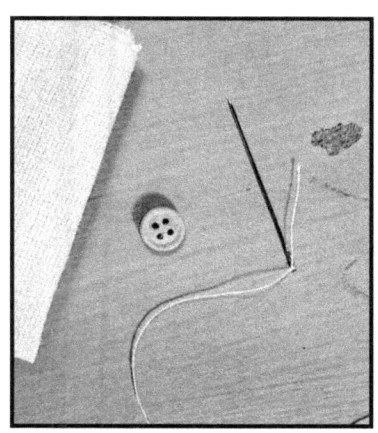

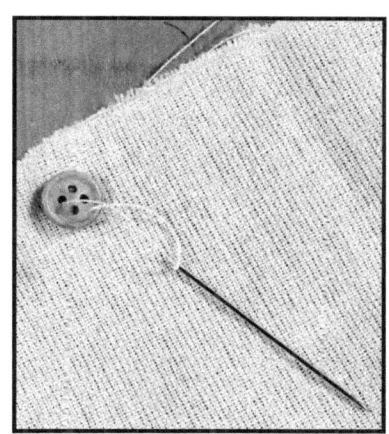

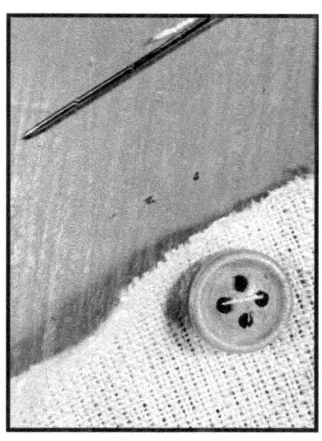

1. Cut off 10-12 inches of thread, and thread the needle. Knot the thread onto the needle head, and tie a knot on the end of the thread strand.

2. Place the button. Entering from the back of the fabric, pull the threaded needle through one of the button holes. Pull all the way through to the point where it is stable but not overly tight.

3. Insert the needle (from front to back) into the opposite hole in the button from the one just used.

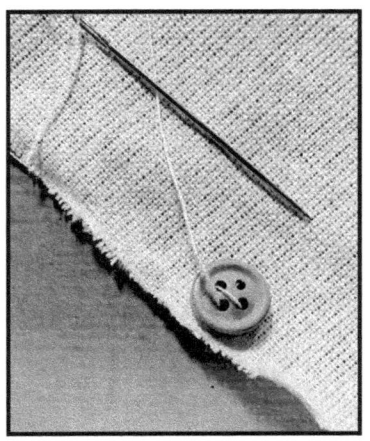 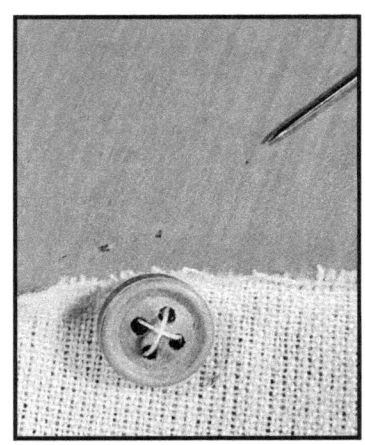 

4. Pull your needle from back to front through another button hole that has not been previously used.

5. Insert the needle into the last button hole from front to back.

6. Repeat steps 2-5 until the button is secure and stable, making sure the button can still be manipulated into a true button hole on a garment if it were needed.

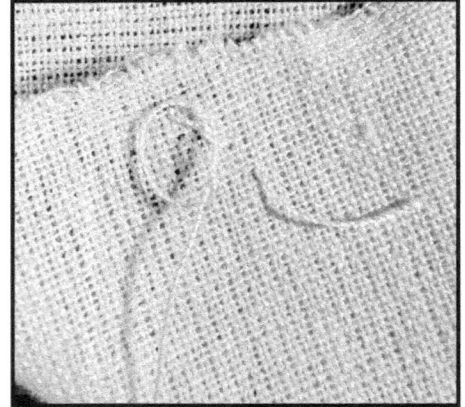

7. On the back, knot the remaining thread, and cut the excess thread.

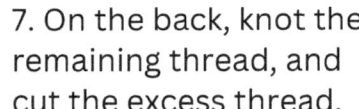

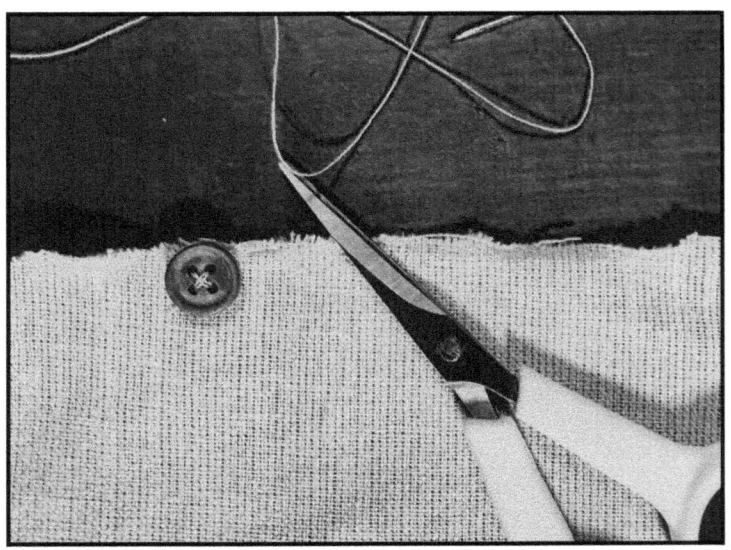

Whether you or your (future) husband and children one day need a button fixed, you now have all the skills you need to continue the life of a piece of clothing.

Take some time and meditate on this word. How would you describe it? What does it mean to you? What do you think of when you hear it? What do you know about it? Categorize your thoughts and feelings about this word in the columns below.

Positives | ## Negatives

"Because of the grace given me by God to be a
minister of Christ Jesus..."
(Romans 15:15-16)

<u>Seek, Love, Trust, Surrender</u>
by Fr. Patrick O'Brien

Trust in God's will and always put Him first in your lives. This begins with seeking relationships that help grow your Faith. It would be well for us to remember that God is all-powerful, all-loving, and all-forgiving. Jesus made it very clear when he was here on earth and said 'whose sins you shall forgive, they are forgiven'. We all have differences.

Rather than holding a grudge, forgive each other as God forgives us.
Prayer is an essential part of our lives and relationships. Jesus said, 'Ask and you shall receive". In our world today, we don't take as much care of each other as we should or give as much time to each other as we should. Husbands and wives must be there for each other in good times and difficult times. Treasure your marriage vows. If you are blessed with children, take care of them together, as they are God's gift to you.

We live in a very busy world these days. Take time for each other. Set aside time to reflect on your relationship. As you lay down to go to sleep each night, ask yourselves, "Were we as good and kind to each other today as we could have been?" There is an old Irish saying, "You never miss your mother until she is buried beneath the clay". It is the same with your spouse. Treasure your time together.

Faith centered friendships and marriages are gifts from God. Pray for each other each day and thank Him for your many blessings.

May God bless and keep you and always hold you in the palm of his hand.

I believe...

God

LOVES

ME

Sign Your Name Here:_____

Key

Redemptive Suffering

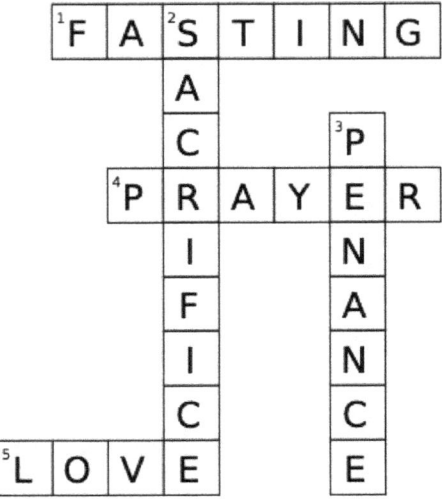

```
¹F A ²S T I N G
      A
      C          ³P
   ⁴P R A Y E R
      I          N
      F          A
      I          N
      C          C
   ⁵L O V E      E
```

Physical Intimacy

```
N N H V M S H G D W P P M G B E U A R M V D F U F B Z P N G
O H L S D Q I L C T I W O I I J N L G B J T B A Q C Z Q A Q
F F B V V W C J P U N C Z T Z F M U P U Z O E E P U U L O P
X D K M I V F C T K D C Q T R E C C M W Z P B U E N Y J V E
U A O B N A F G F C I W Y F Y S V S I L M A S N O I S N Q K
U H U L C K J A L M V O F O I I M M O R F W K I M T T Y D N
Z V R L B F N D J N E W Q B S Y W O Y W G H Q S I I J O P
E U S R G X J R P W L Y W B A L G F M X T E W U B V W W M Y
S X I E D X K Q S H F A P D L R O T H Y S Z W E S E O N Z A
E E A F M O M L J R E N E W A L O F V O W S K E L Y S Q M D
T W L U M K X J A M L P H U F A Q V S O J M N X C S J N Q W
U Y K F O R V A R U J Y R L N L O S P V X Z Y P V N Q P T Y
T O A H G D C S L T P D R W T O V V R P R O C R E A T I V E
F Y G Q P I M Q I U S L U N X V H D S F P F J E K V Q X J N
W T L E D U V W Y A K S G M K E K M E P N U L S G D A S V S
V B Z B O K R I E L F V B P J I J J J B Z T C S K K R R N Q
R H G E K S C V N A X S R C X B L P G V U Y G I X Q N I T V
B N D Q H T X Q U G M C N G E C X B L M S G S O M H D L S O
S P Y G Z S P I R I T U A L C O M M U N I O N N V Q L I B Q
J V Y N V U T R V A M X T X X Z D T D N A A E O N J S U J A
F E D I A A D C D G Y C L Y K N G M I D W U A F L R A N X E
G D J Q E K K E S C U G N E C T N G I J J I L D M S G K Y G J
N D I V P E I W T X W P Y P F I S B G D B G H A G R I P H E
T C B D V K G X E X C S B B R B M V K W O T C R A S D H M W
A N G W H N D A J R C W T D A W J N V M H U W R D C E P I H
O O P T K S W G T J A B M M Y I L J W K N W O I L R Y Y B Y
S N Y J V N V F O U F E S M F Z P F S V W H O A M O R P P M
J F H M S Y N K F X V O Y V Y W T C K T D C E G W E L A E P
W E O I E E P C X J E R J W C S Q Z S M Z I G E G W H V B R
F E O A U U B D X F J Q Y E I R C I J F X U E T Y T K L T R
```

Key

5 "Whoever is without love does not know God, for God is love."

8 "Do even the smallest things out of great love."

2 "The fear of God prepares a place for love."

4 "My soul proclaims the greatness of the Lord."

6 "Love is always only 'becoming.'"

7 "We become what we love and who we love shapes what we become."

1 "To love is to will the good of the other."

3 "Love is shown more in deeds than in words."

1. St. Thomas Aquinas, Summa Theologica
2. St. Augustine, Ninth Homily on 1 John, 4
3. St. Ignatius of Loyola
4. Our Blessed Mother, Luke 1: 46

5. John 4:8
6. Pope St. John Paul II
7. St. Clare of Assisi
8. St. Faustina

Dear Sister In Christ,

You did it! You have completed the *Veiled* workbook.

As I was putting the finishing touches on this workbook, my sister, Yzzy, sent me a picture of this. It caught her eye from the ground of her church's parking lot. I took it as a sign to share it with you. It's true. You are NOT alone.

He is with you in every second of every minute of every hour of every single day. He is with you in the darkest moments of your life and with you in the most joyful ones. He is there in the ordinary and there in the extraordinary.

Our Lord is with you **ALWAYS**.

I hope this time we have spent together has been fruitful for you. I pray that it has been a time of reflection, of growth, of peace, of hope, and most importantly, of love!

You are **SO LOVED**!

Your (future) marriage and motherhood are outward reflections of our Lord's indescribable, transcendent love. They are sacred, and they are holy. They were designed by the almighty and ever-powerful God for *you* to participate in His creation and love.

Our God is veiled in truth, goodness, and beauty, and so are you because you are made in His image and likeness! Yes, you, dear sister.

You are called to be a **SAINT**! We all are.

You will forever be in my prayers. Please pray for me too.

With all my love,

Kira

Acknowledgements

There are many people I could thank in this section, but alas, it would take pages and pages to adequately thank everyone who influenced the making of this workbook.

First, I will start by thanking the eight priests who wrote articles. They graciously accepted my invitation to contribute, without quite realizing that it meant that I would haunt them with reminders until their articles were complete. When I explained my vision for their accompaniment and guidance in this conversation, every single one of them was more than willing to take time out of their full priestly lives to be of service. What gratitude we should all have for our earthly shepherds!

Next, I would like to thank Leigh Ebberwein for her beautiful foreward and helpful feedback during the drafting phase. As close family friends, Leigh and her husband, John, were some of the first people to hold me as a baby. They are and have been beautiful witnesses to the truth and goodness of faith and love in marriage and family life to us our entire lives.

I want to also extend a thank you to Andie Andrews Eisenberg, author of *Farming and Homesteading with the Saints*, for being the first to suggest that a curriculum was needed to accompany my book, *Veiled In Goodness*. At the time, I was only four chapters in on *VIG*, and I couldn't even fathom the idea of actually completing one book just to start another one that seemed even more daunting. Her words rang true, though, when, six months later, the principal at St. Vincent's Academy called me as I pulled away from school on the last day to pitch the idea of me creating a curriculum to return with the following year.

Which brings me to thanking Dawn Odom, Diana Tuten, and Mary Anne Hogan at St. Vincent's Academy for their faith in this program, in me, and in their students. Their fervor for educating the entire personhood of the young women in their care is admirable and inspiring.

Of course, I'd be remiss without formally thanking Our Lady and the Holy Spirit for guiding my pen, so to speak, for all of this. There was a moment in July 2024, with the countdown to the school year dwindling and the pages of the workbook left blank, when I officially surrendered the workbook to Our Lady. If it was going to be made, she had to write it because I didn't even know where to begin. At 10:30 that night, I sat in tears at the immensity of the task, begging her to help me. Twenty minutes later, as I went to turn off the lights, the entire layout of the workbook almost knocked me out with how forcefully it entered my brain. I immediately grabbed my laptop and got to work. Three hours later, half of the workbook was complete, and I went to sleep full of gratitude.

As always, thank you to my husband and my children, who were ever patient and loving with me when I completely zoned out while creating this.

And, thank you, dear participant! This was all made for you and your walk with God. Thank you for pausing your busy life to take the time to look at Him. He's always looking at you, and He loves you!

www.ingramcontent.com/pod-product-compliance
Lightning Source LLC
Chambersburg PA
CBHW041144120626
46547CB00020B/3103